T0329376

THE

PANAMA CANAL CONFLICT

BETWEEN

GREAT BRITAIN

AND

THE UNITED STATES OF AMERICA.

THE
PANAMA CANAL CONFLICT

BETWEEN

GREAT BRITAIN

AND

THE UNITED STATES OF AMERICA

A STUDY

BY

L. OPPENHEIM, M.A., LL.D.

Whewell Professor of International Law in the University of Cambridge
Honorary Member of the Royal Academy of Jurisprudence at Madrid
Member of the Institute of International Law

SECOND EDITION

Cambridge:
at the University Press

1913

CAMBRIDGE
UNIVERSITY PRESS

University Printing House, Cambridge CB2 8BS, United Kingdom

Published in the United States of America by Cambridge University Press, New York

Cambridge University Press is part of the University of Cambridge.

It furthers the University's mission by disseminating knowledge in the pursuit of education, learning and research at the highest international levels of excellence.

www.cambridge.org
Information on this title: www.cambridge.org/9781107418790

© Cambridge University Press 1913

First published 1913
First paperback edition 2014

A catalogue record for this publication is available from the British Library

ISBN 978-1-107-41879-0 Paperback

PREFACE TO THE SECOND EDITION

TO my great surprise, the publishers inform me that the first edition of my modest study on the Panama Canal conflict between Great Britain and the United States is already out of print and that a second edition is at once required. As this study had been written before the diplomatic correspondence in the matter was available, the idea is tempting now to re-write the essay taking into account the arguments proferred in Sir Edward Grey's despatch to the British Ambassador at Washington of November 14, 1912—see Parliamentary Paper Cd. 6451—and, in answer thereto, in Mr Knox's despatch to the American Chargé d'Affaires in London of January 17, 1913—see Parliamentary Paper Cd. 6585. But apart from the fact that the immediate need of a second edition does not permit me time to re-write the work, it seemed advisable to reprint the study in its original form, correcting only some misprints and leaving out the footnote on page 5. It had been written *sine ira et studio* and without further information than that which could be gathered from the Clayton-Bulwer Treaty, the Hay-Pauncefote Treaty, the Hay-Varilla Treaty, the Panama Canal Act, and the Memorandum which President Taft left when signing that Act. Hence, the reader is presented with a study which is absolutely independent of the diplomatic correspondence, and he can exercise his own judgment in comparing my arguments with those set forth *pro et contra* the British interpretation of the Hay-Pauncefote Treaty in the despatches of Sir Edward Grey and Mr Knox.

L. O.

CAMBRIDGE,
    February 15, 1913.

CONTENTS

I.

The Panama Canal conflict is due to the fact that the Governments of Great Britain and the United States do not agree upon the interpretation of Article III, No. 1, of the Hay-Pauncefote Treaty of September 18, 1901, which stipulates as follows:—

> "The Canal shall be free and open to the vessels of commerce and of war of all nations..., on terms of entire equality, so that there shall be no discrimination against any such nation, or its citizens or subjects, in respect of the conditions and charges of traffic, or otherwise. Such conditions and charges of traffic shall be just and equitable."

By Section 5 of the Panama Canal Act of August 24, 1912, the President of the United States is authorised to prescribe, and from time to time to change, the tolls to be levied upon vessels using the Panama Canal, but the section orders that *no tolls whatever shall be levied upon vessels engaged in the coasting trade of the United States*, and also that, if the tolls to be charged should be based upon net registered tonnage for ships of commerce, the tolls shall not exceed one dollar and twenty-five cents per net registered ton nor be less, *for other vessels than those of the United States or her citizens*, than the estimated proportionate cost of the actual maintenance and operation of the Canal[1].

Now Great Britain asserts that since these enactments set forth in Section 5 of the Panama Canal Act are in favour of vessels of the United States, they comprise

[1] As regards the enactment of Section 5 of the Panama Canal Act that the vessels of the Republic of Panama shall be entirely exempt from the payment of tolls, see below IX, p. 48.

a violation of Article III, No. 1, of the Hay-Pauncefote Treaty which stipulates that the vessels of all nations shall be treated on terms of entire equality.

This assertion made by Great Britain is met by the Memorandum which, when signing the Panama Canal Act, President Taft left to accompany the Act. The President contends that, in view of the fact that the Panama Canal has been constructed by the United States wholly at her own cost, upon territory ceded to her by the Republic of Panama, the United States possesses the power to allow her own vessels to use the Canal upon *such terms as she sees fit*, and that she may, therefore, permit her vessels to pass through the Canal either without the payment of any tolls, or on payment of lower tolls than those levied upon foreign vessels, and that she may remit to her own vessels any tolls which may have been levied upon them for the use of the Canal. The President denies that Article III, No. 1, of the Hay-Pauncefote Treaty can be invoked against such power of the United States, and he contends that this Article III was adopted by the United States for a specific purpose, namely, as a basis of the neutralisation of the Canal, and for no other purpose. This article, the President says, is a declaration of policy by the United States that the Canal shall be neutral; that the attitude of the Government of the United States is that all nations will be treated alike and no discrimination is to be made against any one of them observing the five conditions enumerated in Article III, Nos. 2—6. The right to the use of the Canal and to equality of treatment in the use depends upon the observance of the conditions by the nations to whom the United States has extended that privilege. The privileges of all nations to which the use of the Canal has been granted subject to the observance of the conditions for its use, are to be equal to the privileges granted to any one of them which observes those conditions. In other words—so the President continues— the privilege to use the Canal is a conditional most-favoured-nation treatment, the measure of which, in the absence of an express stipulation to that effect, is not what the United States gives to her own subjects, but the treatment to which she submits other nations.

From these arguments of the President it becomes apparent that the United States interprets Article III, No. 1, of the Hay-Pauncefote Treaty as stipulating no discrimination against *foreign* nations, but as leaving it open to her to grant any privilege she likes to her own vessels. According to this interpretation, the rules for the use of the Canal are merely a basis of the neutrality which the United States was willing should be characteristic of the Canal, and are not intended to limit or hamper the United States in the exercise of her sovereign power in dealing with her own commerce or in using her own Canal in whatever manner she sees fit. The President specifically claims the right of the United States eventually to allow her own vessels to use the Canal without the payment of any tolls whatever, for the reason that foreign States could not be prevented from refunding to their vessels tolls levied upon them for the use of the Canal. If foreign States, but not the United States, had a right to do this—so the President argues—the irresistible conclusion would be that the United States, although she owns, controls, and has paid for the construction of the Canal, is restricted by the Hay-Pauncefote Treaty from aiding her own commerce in a way open to all other nations. Since the rules of the Hay-Pauncefote Treaty did not provide, as a condition for the privilege of the use of the Canal upon equal terms with other nations, that other nations desiring to build up a particular trade, involving the use of the Canal, should neither directly agree to pay the tolls nor refund to their vessels tolls levied, it is evident that the Hay-Pauncefote Treaty does not affect the right of the United States to refund tolls to her vessels, unless it is claimed that rules ensuring all nations against discrimination

would authorise the United States to require
that no foreign nation should grant to its
shipping larger subsidies or more liberal
inducements to use the Canal than were
granted by any other nation.

II.

It cannot be denied that at the first
glance the arguments of the United States
appear to be somewhat convincing. On
further consideration, however, one is struck
by the fact that the whole argumentation
starts from, and is based upon, an absolutely
wrong presupposition, namely, that the United
States is not in any way restricted by the Hay-
Pauncefote Treaty with regard to the Panama
Canal, but has granted to foreign nations
the use of the Canal under a conditional
most-favoured-nation clause.

This presupposition in no way agrees with
the historical facts. When the conclusion of

the Hay-Pauncefote Treaty was under consideration, in 1901, the United States had not made the Canal, indeed did not own the territory through which the Canal has now been made; nor was the United States at that time absolutely unfettered with regard to the projected Canal, for she was bound by the stipulations of the Clayton-Bulwer Treaty of 1850. Under this treaty she was bound by more onerous conditions with regard to a future Panama Canal than she is now under the Hay-Pauncefote Treaty. Since she did not own the Canal territory and had not made the Canal at the time when she agreed with Great Britain upon the Hay-Pauncefote Treaty, she ought not to maintain that she granted to foreign nations the privilege of using *her* Canal under a conditional most-favoured-nation clause, she herself remaining unfettered with regard to the conditions under which she could allow her own vessels the use of the Canal. The historical facts are five in number:—

Firstly, in 1850, Great Britain and the

United States, by the Clayton-Bulwer Treaty, agreed that neither of them would ever obtain or maintain for herself any exclusive control over a future Panama Canal, or fortify it, or occupy or colonise any part of Central America; that the Canal should be neutralised, should be open to the vessels of all nations under conditions of equality; and so forth.

Secondly, in 1901, the two parties to the Clayton Bulwer Treaty agreed to substitute for it the Hay-Pauncefote Treaty, Article II of which expressly stipulates *inter alia* that the Canal may be constructed under the auspices of the Government of the United States and that the said Government, *subject to the provisions of Articles III and IV*, shall have the exclusive right of providing for the regulation and management of the Canal.

Thirdly, the parties agreed—see the preamble of the Hay-Pauncefote Treaty—that the general principle of the neutralisation of the Canal as established by the Clayton-Bulwer Treaty should not be impaired, and that, therefore, the United States—see Article III of the Hay-Pauncefote Treaty—agrees to adopt as the basis of the neutralisation of the Canal certain rules, substantially the same as those embodied in the Suez Canal Convention of 1888, and amongst these a rule concerning the use of the Canal by vessels of all nations on terms of entire equality without discrimination against any such nation, or their citizens or subjects, in respect of the conditions or charges of traffic, or otherwise, such conditions and charges to be just and equitable.

Fourthly, the parties agreed—see Article IV of the Hay-Pauncefote Treaty—that no change of the territorial sovereignty or of the international relations of the country or countries traversed by the future Canal should affect the general principle of the neutralisation or the obligation of the parties under the Hay-Pauncefote Treaty.

Fifthly, when, in 1903, the United States by the Hay-Varilla Treaty, acquired from the Republic of Panama the strip of territory necessary for the construction, administration, and protection of the Canal, she acquired sovereign rights over this territory and the future Canal *subject to the antecedent restrictions imposed upon her by the Hay-Pauncefote Treaty*, for Article IV of the latter stipulates expressly that *no* change of territorial sovereignty over the territory concerned shall affect the neutralisation or obligation of the parties *under the treaty*.

These are the unshakable historical facts. The United States did not *first* become the sovereign of the Canal territory and make the Canal, and *afterwards* grant to foreign nations the privilege of using the Canal under certain conditions. No, she has never possessed the power of refusing to grant the use of the Canal to vessels of foreign nations on terms of entire equality, should she ever make the Canal. Free navigation through the Canal for vessels of all nations on terms of entire equality, provided these nations were ready to recognise the neutrality of the Canal, was stipulated by the Clayton-Bulwer Treaty, and this stipulation was essentially upheld by the Hay-Pauncefote Treaty, and it was not until two years after the conclusion of the Hay-Pauncefote Treaty that the United States acquired sovereign rights over the Canal territory and made preparations for the construction of the Canal. For this reason the contention of the United States that she has granted to foreign nations the use of the Canal under certain conditions and that such grant includes a conditional most-favoured-nation treatment, is absolutely baseless and out of place. She has not granted anything, the free use of the Canal by vessels of all nations having been the condition under which Great Britain consented to the abrogation of the Clayton-Bulwer Treaty and to the stipulation of Article II of the Hay-Pauncefote Treaty according to which—in contradistinction to Article I of the Clayton-Bulwer Treaty—the United States is allowed to have a canal constructed under her auspices.

III.

If the assertion of the United States that she herself is entirely unfettered in the use of the Canal, and that the conditions imposed upon foreign vessels in return for the privilege of using the Canal involve a most-favoured-nation treatment, were correct, the United States would not be bound to submit to the rules laid down by Article III, Nos 2—6, of the Hay-Pauncefote Treaty. She could, therefore, if she were a belligerent, commit acts of hostility in the Canal against vessels of her opponent; could let her own men-of-war revictual or take in stores within the Canal even if there were no strict necessity for doing so; could embark and disembark troops, munitions of war, or warlike materials in the Canal, although all these were destined to be made use of during the war generally, and not only for the defence of the Canal against a possible attack. There ought, however, to be no doubt that the

United States is as much bound to obey the
rules of Article III of the Hay-Pauncefote
Treaty as Great Britain or any other foreign
State. These rules are intended to invest
the Canal with the character of neutrality.
If the United States were not bound to obey
them, the Canal would lose its neutral
character, and, in case she were a belligerent,
her opponent would be justified in consider-
ing the Canal a part of the region of war
and could, therefore, make it the theatre of
war. The mere fact that Article III of the
Hay-Pauncefote Treaty refers to the rules
in existence concerning the neutralisation of
the Suez Canal, and that Article IV of the
Suez Canal Treaty of 1888 expressly stipulates the neutralisation of the Canal even
should Turkey be a belligerent, ought to be
sufficient to prove that the neutralisation of
the Panama Canal is stipulated by the Hay-
Pauncefote Treaty even should the United
States be a belligerent.

Furthermore, one must come to the same
conclusion if one takes into consideration

the objects, which are three in number, of the neutralisation of an inter-oceanic canal.

The first object is that a canal shall be open in time of war as well as in time of peace, so that navigation through the canal may be unhampered by the fact that war is being waged. If the canal were not neutralised, the territorial sovereign would be compelled, if he were neutral in a war, to prevent the passing through the canal of men-of-war of either belligerent, because such passage would be equivalent to the passage of belligerent troops through neutral land territory.

The second object is that the territorial sovereign shall be prevented from closing a canal or interfering with the free use of it by vessels of all nations in case he himself is a party to a war. If the canal were not neutralised, the belligerent territorial sovereign could, during the war, close the canal or interfere with its free use by neutral vessels.

The third object is that a canal shall not be damaged, nor navigation thereon be prevented or hampered by the opponent in case the territorial sovereign is himself a belligerent. If the canal were not neutralised, it could be blockaded, militarily occupied, and hostilities could be committed there.

With these points in mind one may well ask whether it was worth while to agree at all upon the five rules of Article III, Nos. 2—6, of the Hay-Pauncefote Treaty if the United States were not to be considered bound by these rules. That two years after the conclusion of the Hay-Pauncefote Treaty the United States acquired sovereign rights over the Canal territory and that she is at present the owner of the Canal has not, essentially at any rate, altered the case, for Article IV of the Hay-Pauncefote Treaty stipulates that a change of territorial sovereignty over the Canal territory should not affect the obligation of the contracting parties under that treaty.

If this is correct, it might be maintained that the United States is, under the Hay-Pauncefote Treaty, subjected to more onerous conditions than Turkey and Egypt are under the Suez Canal Treaty, for Article X of the latter stipulates that Egypt and Turkey shall not by the injunctions of Articles IV, V, VII, and VIII of the same treaty be considered to be prevented from taking such measures as might be necessary to ensure the defence of Egypt and Turkey by their own armed forces. But this opinion would not be justified because in this respect the case of the Panama Canal is entirely different from that of the Suez Canal. Whereas the Panama Canal is an outlying part of the United States, and no attack on the main territory of the United States is possible from the Panama Canal, an attack on Egypt as well as on Turkey is quite possible from the Suez Canal. There is, therefore, no occasion for the United States to take such measures in the Panama Canal as might be necessary to ensure the defence of her main territory. Indeed there might be occasion for her to take such measures in the Canal as are necessary to ensure the defence of the Canal and the surrounding territory, if a belligerent threatened to attack it. Although this case is not directly provided for by the Hay-Pauncefote Treaty—in contradistinction to Article XXIII of the Hay-Varilla Treaty—there is no doubt that, since, according to Article II of the Hay-Pauncefote Treaty, the United States shall have and enjoy all the rights incident to the construction of the Canal as well as the exclusive right of providing for the regulation and management of the Canal, there is thereby indirectly recognised the power of the United States to take all such measures as might become necessary for the defence of the Canal against a threatening attack. Apart from this case, the United States, even if she herself were a belligerent, has no more rights in the use of the Canal than her opponent or a neutral Power; on the contrary she is as much bound as these Powers to submit to the rules of Article III, Nos. 2—6, of the Hay-Pauncefote Treaty.

IV.

However this may be, the question as to whether the stipulation of Article III, No. 1, of the Hay-Pauncefote Treaty that vessels of all nations shall be treated on the basis of entire equality is meant to apply to vessels of all nations without exception, or only to the vessels of *foreign* nations and not to those of the United States, can only be decided by an interpretation of Article III which takes the whole of the Hay-Pauncefote Treaty as well as the Clayton-Bulwer Treaty into consideration.

(1) There is no doubt that according to the Clayton-Bulwer Treaty the future Canal was to be open on like terms to the citizens of all nations including those of the United States, for Article VIII expressly stipulates "that the same canals or railways, being open to the subjects and citizens of Great Britain

and the United States on equal terms, shall also be open on like terms to the subjects and citizens of every other State which...."

(2) The Clayton-Bulwer Treaty has indeed been superseded by the Hay-Pauncefote Treaty, but it is of importance to notice the two facts, expressed in the preamble of the latter:—(*a*) that the only motive for the substitution of the latter for the former treaty was to remove any objection which might arise under the Clayton-Bulwer Treaty to the construction of the Canal under the auspices of the Government of the United States; (*b*) that it was agreed that the general principle of neutralisation as established by Article VIII of the Clayton-Bulwer Treaty should not be considered to be impaired by the new treaty. Now the equal treatment of American, British, and any other nation's vessels which use the Canal is part and parcel of the general principle of neutralisation as established by Article VIII of the Clayton-Bulwer Treaty, and such equal treatment must, therefore, be considered

not to have been impaired by Article III of the Hay-Pauncefote Treaty.

(3) Article III of the Hay-Pauncefote Treaty stipulates—as a consequence of the fact, expressed in the preamble of the Treaty, that the general principle of neutralisation of the Canal as established by Article VIII of the Clayton-Bulwer Treaty shall not be impaired by the Hay-Pauncefote Treaty—that the United States adopts, as the basis of the neutralisation of the Canal, six rules *sub stantially as embodied in the Suez Canal Treaty of Constantinople of* 1888. Now although the Suez Canal Treaty nowhere directly lays down a rule which is identical with the rule of Article III, No. 1, of the Hay-Pauncefote Treaty, it nevertheless insists upon equal treatment of the vessels of all nations by stating in Article XII:—"The high contracting parties, *in application of the principle of equality concerning the free use of the canal, a principle which forms one of the bases of the present treaty,* agree that...." That this principle of equality of

all nations concerning the free use of the
Suez Canal means equality of vessels of all
nations with the exception of the vessels of
Egypt or even of Turkey, has never been
contended; such a contention would, I am
sure, have been objected to by the parties
to the Suez Canal Treaty. For this reason
the term "all nations" in the Hay-Pauncefote
Treaty can likewise only mean *all* nations,
including the United States.

(4) The literal meaning of the words "all
nations" leads to the same conclusion. If
something is stipulated with regard to "all"
nations, every nation is meant without exception. If an exception had been contemplated, the words "all nations" could not have
been used, and if all foreign nations only were
contemplated, the words "all foreign nations"
would have been made use of.

(5) There is also an argument from Article IV of the Hay-Pauncefote Treaty which
states that no change of territorial sovereignty
or of the international relations of the country
or countries traversed by the Canal should

affect the general principle of neutralisation or the obligation of the high contracting parties under the treaty. The general principle of neutralisation is, as laid down in the preamble of the Hay-Pauncefote Treaty, the general principle of neutralisation as established by Article VIII of the Clayton-Bulwer Treaty, and it has already been shown—see above IV, No. 2, p. 24—that equal treatment of British, American, and any other nation's vessels using the Canal is part and parcel of that general principle of neutralisation.

(6) Lastly, Article IV of the Hay-Pauncefote Treaty must be read in conjunction with Article II. The latter does not exclusively contemplate the construction of the Canal by the United States, it contemplates rather the construction *under the auspices of the United States, either* directly at her cost, *or* by gift or loan of money to individuals or corporations, *or* through subscription to or purchase of stocks and shares. The question may well be asked whether, in case the United States had not acquired the Canal

territory and had not herself made the Canal, but had enabled a company to construct it by the grant of a loan, or by taking shares, and the like, she would then also have interpreted the words "all nations" to mean "all foreign nations," and would, therefore, have claimed the right to insist upon her own vessels enjoying such privileges in the use of the Canal as need not be granted to vessels of other nations. Can there be any doubt that she would *not* have done it? And if we can reasonably presume that she would not have done it under those conditions, she cannot do it now after having acquired the Canal territory and having herself made the Canal, for Article IV declares that a change in the territorial sovereignty of the Canal territory shall neither affect the general principle of neutralisation nor the obligation of the parties under the treaty.

V.

I have hitherto only argued against the contention of President Taft that the words "all nations" mean all foreign nations, and that, therefore, the United States could grant to her vessels privileges which need not be granted to vessels of other States using the Panama Canal. For the present the United States does not intend to do this, although Section 5 of the Panama Canal Act—see above I, p. 6—empowers the President to do it within certain limits. For the present the Panama Canal Act exempts only vessels engaged in the American coasting trade from the payment of tolls, and the memorandum of President Taft maintains that this exemption does not discriminate against foreign vessels since these, according to American Municipal Law, are entirely excluded from the American coasting trade and, therefore, cannot be in any way put to a disadvantage through the exemption from the payment of the Canal tolls of American vessels engaged in the American coasting trade.

At the first glance this assertion is plausible, but on further consideration it is seen not to be correct, for the following reasons:—

(1) According to Article III, No. 1, of the Hay-Pauncefote Treaty the charges for the use of the Canal shall be just and equitable. This can only mean that they shall not be higher than the cost of construction, maintenance, and administration of the Canal requires, and that every vessel which uses the Canal shall bear a proportionate part of such cost. Now if all the American vessels engaged in the American coasting trade were exempt from the payment of tolls, the proportionate part of the cost to be borne by other vessels will be higher, and, therefore, the exemption of American coasting trade vessels is a discrimination against other vessels.

(2) The United States gives the term

"coasting trade" a meaning of unheard-of extent which entirely does away with the distinction between the meaning of coasting trade and colonial trade hitherto kept up by all other nations. I have shown in former publications—see the *Law Quarterly Review*, Vol. xxiv (1908), p. 328, and my treatise on International Law, 2nd edition (1912), Vol. i, § 579—that this attitude of the United States is not admissible. But no one denies that any State can exclude foreign vessels not only from its coasting trade, but also from its colonial trade, as, for instance, France, by a law of April 2, 1889, excluded foreign vessels from the trade between French and Algerian ports. I will not, therefore, argue the subject again here, but will only take into consideration the possibility that Great Britain, and some other States, might follow the lead of America and declare all the trade between the mother countries and ports of their colonies to be coasting trade, and exclude foreign vessels therefrom. Would the United States be ready then to exempt coasting trade vessels of foreign States from the payment of Panama tolls in the same way that she has exempted her own coasting trade vessels? If she would not—and who doubts that she would not?—she would certainly discriminate in favour of her own vessels against foreign vessels. Could not the foreign States concerned make the same assertion that is now made by the United States, viz. that, foreign vessels being excluded from their coasting trade, the exemption of their own coasting trade vessels from tolls did not comprise a discrimination against the vessels of other nations? The coasting trade of Russia offers a practical example. By a Ukase of 1897 Russia enacted that trade between any of her ports is to be considered coasting trade, and the trade between St Petersburg and Vladivostock is, therefore, coasting trade from which foreign vessels are excluded. Will the United States, since the Panama Canal Act exempts all American coasting trade vessels from the Panama Canal tolls, be ready to exempt Russian coasting trade vessels likewise? Surely the refusal of such exemption would be a discrimination against Russian in favour of American coasting trade vessels!

(3) The unheard-of extension by the United States of the meaning of the term coasting trade would allow an American vessel sailing from New York to the Hawaiian Islands, but touching at the ports of Mexico or of a South American State, after having passed the Panama Canal, to be considered as engaged in the coasting trade of the United States. Being exempt from paying the Canal tolls she could carry goods from New York to the Mexican and South American ports concerned at cheaper rates than foreign vessels plying between New York and these Mexican and South American ports. There is, therefore, no doubt that in such cases the exemption of American coasting trade vessels from the tolls would involve a discrimination against foreign vessels in favour of vessels of the United States.

(4) It has been asserted that the wording of Article III, No. 1, of the Hay-Pauncefote Treaty only prohibits discrimination *against* some particular nation, and does not prohibit a *special favour to* a particular nation, and that, therefore, special favours to the coasting trade vessels of the United States are not prohibited. But this assertion is unfounded, although the bad drafting of Article III, No. 1, lends some slight assistance to it. The fact that in this article the words "so that there shall be no discrimination against any such nation" are preceded by the words "the canal shall be free and open to the vessels of commerce and of war of all nations observing these rules, *on terms of entire equality*," proves absolutely that any favour to any particular nation is prohibited because it must be considered to involve a discrimination against other nations.

VI.

There is one more contention in the memorandum of President Taft in favour of the assertion that the United States is empowered to exempt all her vessels from the Panama Canal tolls. It is the following:— Since the rules of the Hay-Pauncefote Treaty do not provide, as a condition for the privilege of using the Canal upon equal terms with other nations, that other nations desiring to build up a particular trade which involves the use of the Canal shall not either directly pay the tolls for their vessels or refund to them the tolls levied upon them, the United States could not be prevented from doing the same.

I have no doubt that this contention is correct, but paying the tolls direct for vessels using the Canal or refunding to them the tolls levied is not the same as exempting them from the payment of tolls. Since, as I have shown above in V (1), p. 30, every vessel using the Canal shall, according to Article III, No. 1, of the Hay-Pauncefote Treaty, bear a proportionate part of the cost of construction, maintenance, and administration of the Canal, the proportionate part

of such cost to be borne by foreign vessels
would be higher in case the vessels of the
United States were exempt from the payment of tolls. For this reason the exemption
of American vessels would involve such a
discrimination against foreign vessels as is
not admissible according to Article III, No. 1.

VII.

With regard to the whole question of the
interpretation of Article III of the Hay-
Pauncefote Treaty, the fact is of interest
that prominent members of the American
Senate as well as a great part of the more
influential American Press, at the time the
Panama Canal Act was under the consideration of the Senate, emphatically asserted
that any special privileges to be granted to
American vessels would violate this Article.
President Taft, his advisers, and the majority
of the Senate were of a different opinion,
and for this reason the Panama Canal Act
has become American Municipal Law.

It is likewise of interest to state the fact that the majority of the Senate as constituted thirteen years ago took a different view from the majority of the present Senate, a fact which becomes apparent from an incident in the Senate in December 1900, during the deliberations on the Hay-Pauncefote Treaty of February 5, 1900, the unratified precursor of the Hay-Pauncefote Treaty of November 18, 1901. Senator Bard moved an amendment, namely, that the United States reserves the right in the regulation and management of the Canal to discriminate in respect of the charges of the traffic in favour of vessels of her own citizens engaged in the American coasting trade, but this amendment was rejected by 43 to 27 votes. As Article II, No. 1, of the unratified Hay-Pauncefote Treaty of 1900 comprises a stipulation almost identical with that of Article III, No. 1, of the present Hay-Pauncefote Treaty, there can be no doubt that the Bard amendment endeavoured to secure such a privilege to American coasting trade vessels as the United States now by the Panama Canal Act grants to these vessels. But the Bard amendment was defeated because the majority of the Senate was, in 1900, convinced that it involved a violation of the principle of equality for vessels of all nations pronounced by Article II, No. 1, of the unratified Hay-Pauncefote Treaty of 1900.

VIII.

The conflict concerning the interpretation of the Hay-Pauncefote Treaty throws a flood of light on the practice of the United States respecting the relations between International Law and her Municipal Law.

Two schools may be said to be opposing one another in the science of International Law with regard to the relations between International and Municipal Law.

There are, firstly, a number of publicists who assert that International Law is above Municipal Law and that, therefore, the rules of the former are stronger than the rules of the latter. Accordingly, a Municipal Court would have to apply the rules of International Law whether they are expressly or implicitly recognised by the Municipal Law of the State concerned or not, and even in a case where there is a decided conflict between a rule of Municipal Law and a rule of International Law. "*International Law overrules Municipal Law*" must be said to be the maxim of this school of thought.

There are, secondly, other publicists who maintain that *International Law and Municipal Law are two essentially different bodies of law* which have nothing in common but that they are both branches—but separate branches!—of the tree of Law. The rules of International Law are never, therefore, *per se* part and parcel of the Municipal Law of a State, and a Municipal Court cannot apply the rules of International Law unless they have been adopted, either expressly or implicitly, by the Municipal Law of the State concerned. Should there be a conflict between a rule of International Law and a rule of Municipal Law, a Municipal Court can only apply the rule of Municipal Law, leaving it to the legislature of its State to do away with the conflict by altering the Municipal Law.

I believe that the teaching of the latter school of thought is correct[1] since International and Municipal Law differ as regards their sources, the relations they regulate, and the substance of their law. Rules of International Law can, therefore, only be applied by Municipal Courts in their administration of the law in case and in so far as such rules have been adopted into Municipal Law either by a special Act of the legislature, or by custom, or implicitly.

Now the practice of the Courts[2] of the United States neither agrees with the

---

[1] See my treatise on International Law, 2nd edition (1912), Vol. I, §§ 20—25.

[2] See the account of the practice of the American Courts in Scott's learned article in the *American Journal of International Law*, Vol. I (1908), pp. 856—861.

doctrine of the former nor with the doctrine of the latter school of publicists, but takes a middle line between them. Indeed it considers International Law to be part and parcel of the Municipal Law of the United States. It is, however, far from accepting the maxim that International Law overrules Municipal Law, it accepts rather two maxims, namely, first, that *International Law overrules previous Municipal Law*, and, secondly, that *Municipal Law overrules previous International Law*. In the administration of the law American Courts hold themselves bound to apply the Acts of their legislature even in the case in which the rules of these enactments are not in conformity with rules of previous International Law. It is true that, according to Article VI of the American Constitution, all international treaties of the United States shall be the supreme law of the land, but in case an Act of Congress contains rules not in agreement with stipulations of a previous international treaty, the American Courts consider themselves bound by the Act of Congress, and not by the stipulations of the previous treaty. It is obvious that, according to the practice of the Courts of the United States, International Law and Municipal Law are of *equal* force, so that on the one hand new rules of International Law supersede rules of previous Municipal Law, and, on the other hand, new rules of Municipal Law supersede rules of previous International Law. For this reason, the American Courts cannot be resorted to in order to have the question decided whether or no the enactments of Section 5 of the Panama Canal Act are in conformity with Article III, No. 1, of the Hay-Pauncefote Treaty.

It is a proof of the *bona fides* of President Taft that he desired that the American Courts might be enabled to decide this question. In a message to Congress, dated August 19, 1912, in which the President stated his conviction that the Panama Canal Act under consideration did not violate the Hay-Pauncefote Treaty, he *inter alia* suggested that Congress should pass the following resolution :—

"That nothing contained in the Act, entitled 'An Act to provide for the opening, maintenance, protection, and operation of the Panama Canal, and the sanitation and government of the Canal zone,' shall be deemed to repeal any provision of the Hay-Pauncefote Treaty or to affect the judicial construction thereof, and in any wise to impair any rights or privileges which have been or may be acquired by any foreign nation under the treaties of the United States relative to tolls or other charges for the passage of vessels through the Panama Canal, and that when any alien...... considers that the charging of tolls...... pursuant to the provisions of this Act violates in any way such treaty rights or privileges, such alien shall have the right to bring an action against the United States for redress of the injury which he considers himself to have suffered; and the District Courts of the United States are hereby given jurisdiction to hear and determine such cases, to decree their appropriate relief, and from decision of such District Courts there shall be an appeal by either party to the action of the Supreme Court of the United States."

Congress, however, has not given effect to the suggestion of the President, and the American Courts have not, therefore, the opportunity of giving a judicial interpretation to the Hay-Pauncefote Treaty and of deciding the question whether or no through the Panama Canal Act has arisen a conflict between American Municipal Law and International Law as emanating from the Hay-Pauncefote Treaty.

IX.

It has been asserted that the United States is bound by her general arbitration treaty of April 4, 1908, with Great Britain to

have the dispute concerning the interpretation of the Hay-Pauncefote Treaty decided
by an award of the Permanent Court of
Arbitration at the Hague. It is, however,
not at all certain that this dispute falls under
the British-American Arbitration Treaty.
Article I of this treaty stipulates:—

> "Differences which may arise of a
> legal nature or relating to the interpre-
> tation of treaties existing between the
> two contracting parties and which it may
> not have been possible to settle by
> diplomacy, shall be referred to the Per-
> manent Court of Arbitration established
> at the Hague by the Convention of the
> 29th of July 1899, provided, neverthe-
> less, that they do not affect the vital
> interests, the independence, or the
> honour of the two contracting States,
> *and do not concern the interests of third
> parties.*"

Since this stipulation exempts from obligatory arbitration such differences between
the contracting parties as concern the

interests of third parties, the question
requires an answer whether in the contro-
versial interpretation of the Hay-Pauncefote
Treaty other States than Great Britain and
the United States are interested. The term
interest is, however, a very wide one and so
vague that it is very difficult to decide this
question. Does "interest" mean "rights"?
Or does it mean "advantages"? If it means
"advantages," there is no doubt that in the
Panama Canal conflict the interests of third
parties are concerned, for the free use of the
Canal by their vessels on terms of entire
equality is secured to them by the Hay-
Pauncefote Treaty. On the other hand, if
"interests" means "rights," it can hardly be
said that the interests of third parties are
concerned in the dispute, for the Hay-
Pauncefote Treaty is one to which only
Great Britain and the United States are
contracting parties, and according to the
principle *pacta tertiis nec nocent nec prosunt*
no rights can accrue to third parties from
a treaty. Great Britain has the right to

demand from the United States, which owns and controls the Canal, that she shall keep the Canal open for the use of the vessels of all nations on terms of entire equality, but other States have no right to make the same claim. The case will be different when the Canal has been opened, and has been in use for such length of time as to call into existence—under the influence and working of the Hay-Pauncefote Treaty—a customary rule of International Law according to which the Canal is permanently neutralised and open to vessels of all nations, or when all maritime States, through formal accession to the Hay-Pauncefote Treaty, have entered into it with all rights and duties of the two contracting parties. So long as neither of these events has taken place Great Britain and the United States can at any moment, without the consent of third States, abrogate the Hay-Pauncefote Treaty and do away with the stipulation that the Canal shall be open to vessels of all nations on terms of entire equality.

In this connection it is of interest to draw attention to the fact that, in compliance with Article XIX of the Hay-Varilla Treaty of November 18, 1903, Section 5 of the Panama Canal Act entirely exempts vessels of the Republic of Panama from payment of the Panama Canal tolls. It would seem that this exemption in favour of the vessels of the Republic of Panama violates Article III, No. 1, of the Hay-Pauncefote Treaty, although it is in conformity with Article XIX of the Hay-Varilla Treaty which stipulates that:—

> "The Government of the Republic of Panama shall have the right to transport over the Canal its vessels and its troops and munitions of war in such vessels at all times without paying charges of any kind."

A treaty between two States can never invalidate a stipulation of a previous treaty between one of the contracting parties and a third State. Bearing this point in mind, it must be maintained that the United States, being bound by Article III, No. 1, of the

Hay-Pauncefote Treaty, had not the power to enter into the stipulation of Article XIX of the Hay-Varilla Treaty by which she granted exemption from payment of tolls to vessels of the Republic of Panama, and that Great Britain is justified in protesting against the enactment of Section 5 of the Panama Canal Act in so far as it exempts vessels of Panama from the payment of tolls. The fact that the right of Panama to demand exemption from payment of tolls for her vessels is one of the conditions under which the Republic of Panama ceded to the United States the strip of territory necessary for the construction, administration, and protection of the Canal, cannot invalidate the previously acquired right of Great Britain to demand equal treatment of the vessels of all nations without any exception whatever. It must be left to the United States and the Republic of Panama to come to an agreement concerning Article XIX of the Hay-Varilla Treaty. Although the United States promised an exemption from tolls which she had no power to grant, the Republic of Panama need not drop her claim to this exemption. Since, however, the grant of the exemption would violate previous treaty rights of Great Britain, the Republic of Panama is at any rate entitled to a claim to an equivalent of the exemption, namely, the refunding, on the part of the United States, of tolls paid by vessels of the Republic of Panama for the use of the Canal. Whether these vessels are exempt from the payment of tolls or can demand to have them refunded, makes very little difference to the Republic of Panama, although Article XIX of the Hay-Varilla Treaty stipulates exemption from, and not the refunding of, tolls.

But the case of the vessels of Panama is quite unique, for their exemption from tolls was one of the conditions under which the Republic of Panama ceded to the United States the Canal territory. Great Britain and the United States being the only con-tracting parties to the Hay-Pauncefote Treaty, and third States not having as yet

either by formal accession become parties to
this treaty or acquired, by custom, a claim
to equal treatment of their vessels, there
would seem to be nothing to prevent Great
Britain from consenting to the exemption
of the vessels of Panama, should she be
disposed to do so.

X.

However this may be, the question as to
whether the United States is by the British-
American Arbitration Treaty compelled to
consent to have the dispute concerning the
interpretation of the Hay-Pauncefote Treaty
brought before the Permanent Court of
Arbitration is of minor importance. For,
even if she be not compelled to do so, it
must nevertheless be expected that she
will do so. If any dispute is, by its very
character, fit and destined to be settled by
arbitration, it is this dispute, which is clearly
of a legal nature and at the same time one
which concerns the interpretation of treaties.

Neither the independence, nor the honour, nor any vital interest of the parties can be said to be involved in the dispute.

Indeed it may be maintained that much more important than the dispute itself is the question whether it will or will not be settled by arbitration. Great Britain has already declared that if the dispute cannot be settled by means of diplomacy, she will request arbitration. The eyes of the whole world are directed upon the United States in order to find out her resolution. Throughout her history, the United States has been a champion of arbitration, and no other State has so frequently offered to go, or consented to submit, to arbitration. It was the United States who at the First, as well as the Second, Hague Peace Conference led the party which desired that arbitration should be made obligatory for a number of differences, and she will, I am sure, renew her efforts at the approaching Third Peace Conference. Should she refuse to go to arbitration in her present dispute with Great Britain, the whole movement for arbitration would, for a generation at least, be discredited and come to a standstill. For if the leader of the movement is false to all his declarations and aspirations in the past, the movement itself must be damaged and its opponents must be victorious. Prominent Americans are alive to this indubitable fact, and it would seem to be appropriate to conclude this study with the text of the letter of Mr Thomas Willing Balch of Philadelphia—the worthy son of his father who was the first to demand the settlement of the Alabama dispute by arbitration—which the *New York Sun*, an influential American paper, published on September 4, 1912, on its editorial page.

"To the Editor of the *Sun*. Sir:—

A half century ago, Americans believed firmly that we had a good cause of grievance against Great Britain for having allowed, during our great Civil War, the use of her ports for the fitting out of a fleet of Confederate cruisers, which caused our maritime flag to disappear almost entirely from the high seas. We pressed Great Britain long and persistently to agree that our claims, known under the generic name of the Alabama claims, should be submitted for settlement to an impartial arbitration. Finally, with reluctance, Great Britain acceded to our demands. And as a result the two Nations appeared as litigants before the Bar of the International Court of Justice, popularly known as the Geneva Tribunal. The result was a triumph for the United States, but also it was a greater triumph for the cause of civilization.

To-day our Government and that of Great Britain have once more come to an *impasse*, this time over the interpretation of the Hay-Pauncefote Panama Treaty. Our Government has definitely granted free passage through the Panama Canal to our vessels engaged in the coastwise trade. And as a consequence

Great Britain has entered a protest and given notice that she will request that the Hay-Pauncefote International contract shall be submitted for interpretation to a judicial decision by The Hague Tribunal. Though so short a time has elapsed since the Panama Canal Bill became a law, mutterings have been heard of the possibility that the United States would refuse this request of Great Britain to refer the point in dispute to The Hague Court. But such a policy would be most unwise for the United States to pursue. No better means to injure our foreign trade and relations could be devised. Apart, however, from the material aspect of the question, our national honor and credit would suffer if we refused to refer the matter for judicial settlement at the Bar of The Hague International Court, especially as we have a treaty agreement with Great Britain to refer many forms of possible international dispute to that very tribunal in case ordinary means fail to settle them. In acceding to such a solution of the point of difference between the two Powers, the honor of the United States and Great Britain surely will be as safe in the hands of their respective counsel as the honor of a private individual is in those of his lawyer in a suit before a Municipal Tribunal.

The Alabama Arbitration which involved a large and important part of the rights and duties of neutrals and belligerents towards one another, was a notable advance in strengthening the power and majesty of International Law among the Nations of the world. The present dispute will turn on the correct interpretation of a treaty concerning whose meaning various parties and persons have offered different views. It seems to be clearly a case for a judicial decision.

At the proper time, let the question

be argued before The Hague Court, and whatever the decision may be, which both parties will be pledged in advance to accept, another triumph will have been won for the Law of the Nations. Another step forward—and International Law and Justice can only advance a step at a time—towards the distant goal of universal peace through the expansion of the Law of Nations will be accomplished to the substantial gain and credit of civilization and humanity. And new honor and glory will accrue to the United States, which ever since the signing of Jay's Treaty in 1794 have done so much, probably more than any other Power, to promote the cause of justice among the Nations."

Printed in the United States
By Bookmasters